So Many Ways to Live in
Difficult Conditions

A new way to explore the animal kingdom

Editorial Director
Caroline Fortin

Executive Editor
Martine Podesto

Research and Documentation
Anne-Marie Brault
Kathleen Wynd

Cover Design
Épicentre

Coordination
Lucie Mc Brearty

Page Setup
Chantal Boyer

Executive Illustrator
Jocelyn Gardner

Illustrations
Rielle Lévesque
Marie-Andrée Lemieux (Malem)
Caroline Soucy
Yves Chabot
Raymond Martin
Claude Thivierge
Nicholas Oroc
Danièle Lemay
Richard Blais (Sketch)

Production Manager
Gaétan Forcillo

Translator
Gordon Martin

Copy Editing
Veronica Schami

QUÉBEC AMÉRIQUE

Made-to-measure animals

Heat, water, light and oxygen – these are just some of the ingredients required to sustain life. But certain environments on our planet lack some of the elements living beings need for their development. Burning deserts, freezing ice floes, snow-covered, stormy mountaintops and the darkest depths of the oceans are just some of the environments where inhospitable conditions make it difficult for animals to set up house and home. But that doesn't stop some brave creatures from making their presence felt! They do, however, have to go to extraordinary lengths to adapt to these hostile environments.

Life in slow motion

Firmly suspended by its long curved claws, this strange mammal with a flat, rounded face defies the extreme heat and humidity of the tropical forests of South America. To survive in such conditions, the sloth is careful not to waste any energy at all: it sleeps over 15 hours a day and travels only about 1 kilometer per week! Indistinguishable from the surrounding vegetation, the fur of the sloth is even aligned so that rainwater falls straight to the ground

brown-throated three-toed sloth
Bradypus variegatus

Underwater oases

The barren floor of the deepest depths of the Pacific Ocean contains oases of life: clusters of vents that spit out water from the depths of the Earth. Containing chemical elements of all kinds, this boiling-hot liquid, which can reach temperatures of 400 degrees Celsius, serves as the natural habitat for tube worms. Hidden inside stiff tubes, these invertebrates, which are over 1.5 meters long, live in close association with bacteria that produce the energy-rich compounds the giant worms feed on.

hydrothermal vent tube worm
Riftia pachyptila

Perfect camouflage

There are two types of peppered moths – black ones and white ones. Just a few decades ago, the white moths were more plentiful, but as the coal industry has developed, things have changed dramatically. Concealed on tree trunks covered with soot (coal residue), the black moths easily go unnoticed by their predators. But as for the white ones, well… In response to this change in their habitat, peppered moths now give birth to black offspring that are perfectly adapted to their polluted environment.

peppered moth
Biston betularia

3

Liberated by water

The lungfish, one of the few fish with lungs, can survive even if the stream in which it lives dries up! Thanks to its lungs, it can breathe in the open air, but it has developed an even more extraordinary strategy: buried in the mud, it wraps itself in a cocoon of hardened mucus that protects it for a few months, until a liberating rainfall dissolves its prison and returns the fish to its stream.

lungfish
Protopterus annectens

Are you curious?

Green microscopic algae coat the damp hair of the sloth. Far from inconveniencing the animal, these algae give its fur a green tinge that blends in with the environment of the forest, thus perfecting the camouflage of the mammal.

These ones live in overwhelming heat
surviving under a burning sun

With torrid heat that can reach temperatures of 80 degrees Celsius at the height of day and dry winds that whip up an endless sea of sand, the 49 million square kilometers of hot deserts are undoubtedly the most hostile environments on Earth. Though it is hard to believe that living beings would choose to set up home in such inhospitable conditions, these deserts are home to about 5,000 species of animals, relying on indispensable adaptations for their survival. Seeking at all costs to avoid the burning rays of the sun, some of these animals take refuge underground in relatively cool layers of sand, while others seek respite in the shadows of shrubs or rocks, or in very humid burrows. But some inventive animals have devised incredible survival strategies.

Ship of the desert

The dromedary, or one-humped camel, definitely lives up to its nickname "ship of the desert". First domesticated over 4,000 years ago, this mammal has a unique set of equipment especially adapted for long treks through the desert: hairy ears, eyes with long, thick lashes, and muscular nostrils that can close completely to protect the animal from sandstorms. A reserve of fat on its back provides the dromedary with energy during periods when food and water are scarce.

dromedary
Camelus dromedarius

4

Are you curious?

A great economizer of water, the dromedary not only sweats very little, it also produces dry excrement and just a small amount of urine. After going without water for a long period of time, the dromedary can drink up to 100 liters, which it stores in its body tissue for the difficult times ahead.

Cooling ears

The smallest fox of all eludes the intense desert heat by means of a very unique air-conditioning system. It uses the long, broad ears on its head to eliminate surplus heat from its body. But this little canid has more than one trick up its sleeve. To escape the infernal daytime heat, it spends most of its time 1 meter underground in the coolness of its den.

fennec
Fennecus zerda

The dance of the hot sand

Unlike mammals and birds, reptiles do not have a system that allows them to regulate their body temperature. To prevent its body from getting too hot, the Namib Desert sand dune lizard performs an amusing little dance number. By keeping two feet in the air at all times, this reptile avoids absorbing the burning heat of the desert soil.

Namib Desert sand dune lizard
Aporosaura anchietae

Reservoir frogs

The torrid heat of the Australian deserts is often accompanied by long periods of drought. Buried at a depth of 1 meter, water-holding frogs patiently await the next rain shower. Made up of two distinct layers, their skin spreads apart to form a sort of pocket that fills with water. Protected from dehydration, some of these amphibians lie dormant for up to 5 years without swallowing a single thing!

water-holding frog
Cyclorana platycephalus

These ones live in overwhelming heat
when water runs short

Water is a rare and precious commodity for the inhabitants of the desert. While the tropical rainforests of North America receive up to 3 meters of water per year, the deserts receive an average of barely 2 centimeters. In fact, some deserts remain completely dry for years on end! The inhabitants of the desert must do all they can to conserve water. Some animals almost never have an opportunity to drink, while others make do with the liquid in the food they consume. Certain particularly parsimonious animals quench their thirst by drinking the droplets of moisture secreted by plants or deposited by fog.

Winged sponges

Covering tens of kilometers every day, spotted sandgrouses move around in large groups, which can include hundreds of individuals, in search of water. Crouching in the water, the male sandgrouse shakes its body back and forth, absorbing water droplets it stores in a special cluster of feathers on its belly. Once these feathers are thoroughly soaked with the precious liquid, the male bird returns to its nest to water its offspring.

spotted sandgrouse
Pterocles senegallus

Desert humidifiers

The desert darkling beetle, which is 2.5 centimeters long, is perfectly equipped to confront the harsh climate of the desert. Its thick shell protects its body from the burning rays of the sun. But that's not all! Beneath its hindquarters is a most ingenious device: a chamber that cools and humidifies air before it enters the body of the insect. This portable humidifier allows the darkling beetle to stave off dehydration.

desert darkling beetle
Pimelia retrospinosa

The rat that never drinks

The kangaroo rats of the deserts of North America are the undisputed champions when it comes to saving water! Their food, which consists of dry seeds, leaves and stems, provides the rodents with all the water they need. To retain as much water as possible, the kangaroo rat does not sweat and produces very concentrated urine. It even rechews its droppings, which are as hard as little stones, to remove as much of the moisture from them as possible.

desert kangaroo rat
Dipodomys deserti

Turning fat into water

The spiny-tailed lizard can withstand the droughts of the North African deserts. Hidden beneath the skin on its back is a reserve of fat that serves as a water supply: by means of a chemical transformation, this fat provides water during difficult periods. Extraordinarily resistant to thirst and food shortages, the spiny-tailed lizard never drinks and can go without food for almost a year!

African spiny-tailed lizard
Uromastix acanthinurus

Are you curious?

Female spotted sandgrouses have a sort of pocket on their abdomens made of thick, insulating skin that allows them to lie down on ground that can reach temperatures of 70 degrees Celsius. When the sandgrouse overheats, it pants like a dog.

Some battle and triumph over
frigid temperatures

Numerous animals do constant battle against the cold. From the vast Arctic Ocean to the frozen northern tundra, and in the snow deserts of Antarctica, where the most powerful blizzards on the planet blow, there are a great many habitats on Earth where only the most perfectly acclimatized animals can survive. Can insects possibly survive on ice at temperatures as low as -16 degrees Celsius? Can bats really withstand temperatures of -50 degrees Celsius and can fish tolerate icy water that dips to -2 degrees Celsius? Not only can certain living beings endure the coldest conditions imaginable, some of them are so well adapted that their survival depends on the existence of harsh climates.

The secret of resisting cold

Nice and warm beneath its thick, cosy coat, this pack-forming carnivore can withstand temperatures as low as -70 degrees Celsius! The body of the arctic fox, or white fox, is perfectly adapted to the harsh arctic climate. Between its legs are long hairs that protect its skin from frostbite. Furthermore, very little heat leaves its body by way of its little round ears and short muzzle – extremities normally vulnerable to the cold.

8

arctic fox
Alopex lagopus

An icebound seal

The Weddell seal is the mammal that lives closest to the South Pole, in a hostile environment of ice floes and icy-cold Antarctic waters. Spending almost 8 months of the polar winter in the water, beneath a layer of ice that can be up to 1 meter thick, this seal is well equipped for the cold: its dense fur and a layer of insulating fat about 10 centimeters thick keep it nice and warm.

Weddell seal
Leptonychotes weddelli

Sugar-filled frogs

Concealed under a stone, the North American wood frog is no longer breathing, its blood is no longer flowing through its veins and two-thirds of the water in its body is frozen. Much like a little factory, its body has started to produce substances that will allow it to survive being frozen for several weeks: sugar that supplies energy to its dormant organs and a special antifreeze that prevents ice from forming inside its cells.

wood frog
Rana sylvatica

9

The champion of cold hardiness

A blizzard is raging on the vast arctic tundra. Huddled close together, about 20 musk oxen try to keep themselves warm. These herbivorous mammals of the far north have a great asset that helps them withstand the severe climate: a heavy fur coat that resists cold and moisture. Warmly wrapped up in this thick fleece, musk oxen can withstand temperatures of -70 degrees Celsius.

musk ox
Ovibos moschatus

Are you curious?

Like all mammals and birds, the fox is "homeothermic", meaning it has a control system that allows it to maintain a constant body temperature, no matter what the ambient temperature. "Poikilothermic" animals, such as invertebrates, fish, amphibians and reptiles, do not have this ability.

Some do battle against the cold by
fleeing the rigors of winter

To flee or not to flee? That is the question. Warmly muffled up in a thick layer of fat and wrapped in a thick coat of fur, the best-equipped animals, most of which are large mammals, take on the cold. Others – insects, amphibians and reptiles – surrender to it and freeze to death. Some embark on a long voyage toward regions with warmer climates, while others – dormice, squirrels, hedgehogs and bats – desert the battlefield and fall into a deep sleep, not waking up until the warm days of spring arrive.

The big winter sleep

Cold temperatures, pale sunshine and food shortages signal the beginning of winter: rolled into a ball in its burrow with its head snuggled between its hind legs, the woodchuck settles in for a winter of hibernation. It sleeps in this position from mid-October to mid-March, feeding on the thick layer of fat it has accumulated in preparation for its long restful winter.

woodchuck
Marmota monax

Arctic voyagers

The arctic cold never arrives alone; it is invariably accompanied by food shortages. Without grasses, berries, seeds or aquatic plants to nibble on, the magnificent snow geese of America leave the arctic tundra to seek refuge and food on the prairies of the southern United States and Mexico. But come March, they head back north to reclaim the Arctic.

snow goose
Anser caerulescens

A hibernating turtle

The little painted turtle owes its name to the pretty, colorful designs adorning its shell. This reptile, which can measure between 10 and 25 centimeters, lives in the ponds, lakes and streams of the United States and southern Quebec, feeding on aquatic plants, insect larvae and even small fish. In cold regions, the painted turtle can spend up to 4 months hibernating in a burrow it digs in the mud.

painted turtle
Chrysemys picta

A community refuge

Curled up in the burrow of a rodent, in a crack in a rock or under a tree trunk, about 40 northern European adders hibernate together until the arrival of the mild days of spring. In the fall, when the temperature dips below 9 degrees Celsius, these reptiles retire to their lairs. And in some regions, they remain in seclusion for as long as 275 days! Rolled up and intertwined, the adders conserve their collective body heat.

adder
Vipera berus

11

Are you curious?

During hibernation, the woodchuck lives in slow motion. Its body temperature drops to 8 degrees Celsius, it breathes only about once every 5 minutes and its heart beats just twice per minute. By the time it wakes up, the animal has lost approximately a third of its body weight.

While these ones live in the tranquil depths
of the ocean

One of the darkest environments on Earth is located 2,000 meters beneath the surface of the ocean. Not a single ray of sunshine penetrates the deepest depths of the ocean, and no green plant can survive there. In fact, until the middle of the last century, it was believed that no animal could survive the blackness and isolation of the abysses. However, we now know that many animals live in the heart of this eternal night – at depths of up to 11,000 meters, in the most complete darkness, at an average temperature of 2 degrees Celsius and beneath the enormous weight of a huge mass of water several kilometers thick!

A voracious predator

Equipped with extraordinarily long, fang-like teeth, the viperfish rarely fails to skewer the few prey that frequent the abyssal zone. This monster haunts the temperate and tropical waters of the globe, at depths of between 450 and 2,500 meters. The formidable jaw of the viperfish appears to practically detach itself from the body of the animal, opening wide enough to make a mere mouthful of the shrimp and fish that comprise its diet.

12

viperfish
Chauliodus sloani

A deep-sea-fishing fish

In the impenetrable darkness of the abyssal zone, animals must somehow detect their prey, defend themselves against their predators and distinguish the former from the latter. To do so, most of them rely on a clever means of creating their own light. Some of them even have special spots of light on their belly, sides or head. Using the luminous bacteria on the top of its head, the deep-sea anglerfish lures prey toward its gaping mouth.

deep-sea anglerfish
Himantolophus groenlandicus

The stomach of the murky depths

In the deepest depths of the oceans, food is extremely rare. The beings that live there often have to make do with the plants and dead animals that rain down from higher levels. To deal with this lack of food, the deep-sea gulper eel has developed a unique anatomy: one-quarter of the length of its anguilliform body is made up of an enormous head split by a giant mouth that can swallow a huge quantity of food at once.

deep-sea gulper eel
Eurypharynx pelecanoides

13

The phantom of the depths

Giant squid are not imaginary monsters. They really exist! However, their carcasses are the only evidence of their existence, because no giant squid has ever been seen alive. The largest specimen found to date is 17 meters long. In the darkness of the depths, the enormous eyes of the giant squid, which are almost 40 centimeters in diameter, probably allow the animal to spot its enemies as well as the prey it ensnares in its 11-meter-long tentacles.

giant squid
Architeuthis genus

Are you curious?

The viperfish is a terrible swimmer. It allows itself to be carried by the current until one of its prey happens to drift near its mouth.

these ones lead
very eventful lives!

Life doesn't always flow smoothly for many aquatic creatures. Whipped by powerful waves, tossed about by tides or jostled by strong currents, shellfish, starfish, sea urchins, sea anemones, crustaceans, worms and mollusks cling desperately to life. Nor do animals that live in streams and rivers lead restful lives. Hurtling down rocky mountainsides at dizzying speeds, the cold torrential waters offer little comfort to the animals that venture into them. Yet valiant insects, crustaceans, mollusks and fish take the risk, gripping tightly to stones or hiding under them, or concealing themselves inside a sheath-like casing.

A bird that walks on water

The fast-flowing streams of hills and mountains are the domain of the dipper, which is also known as the water ouzel. The only passerine that leads an amphibious life, this bird finds its food under stones at the bottom of the water. With its tail spread widely, it clings firmly to the streambed with its long claws and walks straight into the current. A skilful diver, it can also swim by tucking its feet against its body and using its wings as fins. Its dives can last for up to 30 seconds!

dipper
Cinclus cinclus

The stream stalker

With its long webbed fingers adapted for swimming, its tail with hairs that serve as a rudder and its impermeable coat, the Szechwan (or Tibetan) water shrew is well equipped to confront the cold, swift waters of Asian streams. Using the suckers on the soles of its feet, the shrew clings to the slippery stones on the streambed and skilfully holds onto the prey it stalks at the bottom of the water.

Szechwan water shrew
Nectogale elegans

saddled hillstream loach
Homaloptera orthogoniata

Current-withstanding suckers

This little 12-centimeter-long, flat-bodied fish has absolutely no fear of the strong currents in the streams of Southeast Asia! Acting somewhat like suckers, the large fins on the belly of the saddled hillstream loach allow it to cling to rocks at the bottom of the water, no matter how strong the current.

The water nymph

The stonefly larva has all the gear required to tackle the icy, turbulent waters of streams and rivers: lungs that allow it to breathe under water, as well as a flat body that does not disrupt the flow of the water and enables the larva to slide under stones. It also has strong claws that allow it to cling firmly to rocks and avoid being carried away by the current. However, this robust little creature is quite picky: it will not live in polluted waters where oxygen is in short supply!

stonefly larva
Plecoptera order

Are you curious?

Thanks to a thick layer of down and very dense plumage, the dipper can withstand temperatures as cold as -45 degrees Celsius! Its skin glands secrete a large quantity of fat that helps make its feathers impermeable.

Some have their heads
in the clouds...

From the Rockies to the Andes, and from the Alps to the Himalayas, thousands of kilometers of mountain ranges are home to all forms of animal life. Braving the cold, powerful gusts of wind, burning sunshine and the threat of avalanches, living beings have ascended the Earth's highest summits. At these dizzying heights, the oxygen that sustains life is a rare commodity: this threatens the survival of many species, but some animals cope quite brilliantly.

The giant of the mountains

Venturing as high as 6,000 metres, this large animal of the mountains of Tibet climbs to altitudes that other mammals will never reach! Trailing on the surfaces of high peaks, its coat of long black hair provides effective protection against the violent winds, while beneath this long hair is an undercoat of short, dense fur that keeps the animal's body warm. With its back to the wind and its head tucked against its front legs, the yak can withstand temperatures as cold as -40 degrees Celsius!

16

yak
Bos grunniens

The climbers' companion

This member of the crow family holds the bird record for survival at the highest altitude. In fact, the air is so thin at very high altitudes that most birds would be unable to remain aloft. But thanks to its long wings, this excellent flier executes skilful aerial maneuvers, performing numerous acrobatic feats and dizzying nosedives. This little champion has been spotted at altitudes as high as 8,000 meters and sometimes accompanies climbers on their ascents to the summit!

Alpine chough
Pyrrhocorax graculus

Mammal of the high plateaus

At altitudes of 4,500 meters, humans have trouble breathing and find the cold temperatures very painful. But, warmly wrapped up in its woolly fur coat, the vicuna runs effortlessly at speeds of over 45 kilometers an hour! With voluminous lungs and blood capable of carrying a large quantity of oxygen, this mammal of the high plateaus, which climbs as high as 5,700 meters, has no reason to fear the rigors of its habitat.

vicuna
Vicugna vicugna

17

Safe eggs

Cold, wind, drought and a lack of oxygen can be hard on the eggs of amphibians, reptiles and insects. But the alpine salamander, which lives at altitudes as high as 3,000 meters, has solved this problem: it keeps its eggs inside its body until they hatch. After a long gestation period that can sometimes last as long as 4 years, the baby salamanders are born, ready to face life's challenges!

alpine salamander
Salamandra atra

Are you curious?

Hemoglobin, a molecule that transports oxygen in the body, functions more efficiently in animals that live at high altitudes than in those that live at sea level: it carries more oxygen.

while others live
in the depths of the Earth

Ever since the great geological upheavals that occurred millions of years ago, some amphibians, fish, insects and other invertebrates have been imprisoned in the darkness, humidity and cold in the bowels of the Earth. Other-worldly in appearance, these strange and unique creatures are perfectly adapted to the darkness, cold temperatures and lack of oxygen in the cavernous depths. Unlike the American porcupine, the cave rat, the bear and certain bats and birds, which visit caves from time to time to rest or to take refuge, troglobites, species that live exclusively in caves, could not survive outside their underground homes.

A blind fish

In the darkness that prevails deep underground, eyes are of absolutely no use! The blind cave tetras found in the caves of Mexico are perfect troglobites. These little fish, which are only a few centimeters long, are born with eyes. But as the young tetras develop, their eyes gradually sink into their heads, until they are completely covered by a layer of skin. Deprived of sight, cave-dwelling species develop their other senses, such as those of touch and smell.

blind cave tetra
Astyanax fasciatus mexicanus

A cave-dwelling amphibian

This strange little creature is undoubtedly the oddest amphibian in the world. Imprisoned in underground rivers and ponds, this 30-centimeter-long salamander has a pinkish, translucent body with three pairs of blood-filled gills, which allow the animal to breathe in the cold underground water. Like most cave-dwelling species, the olm is blind. Buried beneath its skin, its tiny eyes are completely useless.

olm
Proteus anguinus

Darkness-defying radar

All day long, hundreds of oilbirds nest deep within the caves of certain mountainous regions of America. To navigate the interiors of their dark cages, these birds emit the same call over and over again. The speed with which the echo returns tells them how far away the obstacles are. Using this ingenious radar system, the birds fly skilfully through the caves without bouncing off the rocky walls or even getting lost!

oilbird
Steatornis caripensis

19

A lethal light

It is difficult to find anything to eat in the hostile environment of underground streams. To overcome this lack of food, the larva of the fungus gnat has armed itself with a clever trap. Made from sticky threads suspended from the vault of a cave, its lethal weapon ensnares insects attracted by the pretty light produced by the body of the larva.

fungus gnat larva
Arachnocampa luminosa

Are you curious?

Since troglobitic species are not exposed to ultraviolet radiation, their skin does not require the protection provided by pigments. As a result, troglobitic amphibians and fish are translucent: you can see the blood flowing through their pinkish flesh.

While these ones
are in grave danger

The water, air and soil of our planet are polluted. The incredible industrial growth of recent decades has introduced all kinds of pollutants into the environment. Pesticides, herbicides, fertilizers and heavy metals such as mercury and lead have seeped into the soil and polluted the ground, groundwater, lakes, rivers, seas and oceans. The gases produced by the combustion of gasoline and natural gas are responsible for the greenhouse effect, which is making the Earth dangerously hot, and for acid rain, which burns the ground and vegetation. In some parts of the world, many animals are in grave danger.

Fragile shells

Introduced almost 50 years ago, the agricultural pesticide DDT turned out to be a ticking time bomb. The chemical waste found in seawater created a deadly chain reaction: crustaceans whose flesh had been contaminated by DDT were eaten by fish, which in turn poisoned the pelicans that ate them. Female pelicans then began laying eggs with very thin shells. Too fragile, these eggs cracked open before the chicks were ready to emerge.

brown pelican
Pelecanus occidentalis

Seals in a tight spot

The beaches of the Mediterranean Sea were once a paradise for monk seals: there was a complement of almost 5,000 just a few years ago. Today, only 700 seals can be found in the polluted waters of the Mediterranean. On the beaches, the marine mammals have been replaced by sunbathers, underwater divers and motor vehicles. Meanwhile, out at sea, the polluted water is doing irreversible damage to the remaining Mediterranean monk seals.

Mediterranean monk seal
Monachus monachus

Sirens in danger

dugong
Dugong dugong

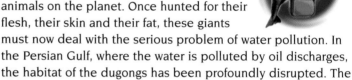

The real-life inspiration for the sirens of Greek legend, these distant relatives of the elephant are among the most endangered animals on the planet. Once hunted for their flesh, their skin and their fat, these giants must now deal with the serious problem of water pollution. In the Persian Gulf, where the water is polluted by oil discharges, the habitat of the dugongs has been profoundly disrupted. The dugong populations still found there may soon become extinct.

Polluted carcasses

With a wingspan of up to 3 meters, the California condor is not only one of the largest birds in the sky but also one of the most endangered. There are only about 50 of these birds left in the world. Many were killed by hunters. Others were poisoned by involuntarily consuming the lead in the bodies of other animals killed by hunters.

California condor
Gymnogyps californianus

Are you curious?

In 1970, the brown pelican was placed on the list of endangered species. Since 1972, the use of DDT has been prohibited. Furthermore, certain islands on which the pelicans nest have been turned into nature preserves. Though still in a precarious situation, the brown pelicans are doing better than before.

While these ones are in grave danger...
disturbed habitats

A quick glance at the world wide situation reveals a distressing picture. Forests are being destroyed at the alarming rate of 200,000 square kilometers per year, and it has been predicted that tropical forests will be wiped out within a few decades. Inundated with water saturated with fertilizer, the fragile coral reefs may become extinct, which will endanger the extraordinarily rich array of animal life that thrives in these calcareous environments. New urban landscapes, roads and buildings are popping up in what once were fields, forests and swamps. Where will the animals go when driven from their homes?

Bad news, bears...

This inhabitant of the wooded mountains of China feeds for 10 hours a day. Its favorite food? Bamboo shoots, of which it consumes 38 kilograms daily! The few isolated groups of pandas that remain are facing a serious problem: the slopes once covered with bamboo have been cleared for cultivation. Furthermore, the valleys inhabited by humans are obstacles to the free movement of pandas, which now number barely 1,000.

giant panda
Ailuropoda melanoleuca

Paradise under threat

Mass colonization combined with the destruction of forests – that is the sad fate of the island of Madagascar, a veritable paradise in the middle of the Indian Ocean. The largest member of the lemur family, the indri lives in the forests on the north-western part of the island, feeding on leaves and fruit. Without access to moist forests, these primates have no chance of survival. At the current rate of deforestation, experts predict that Madagascar will lose all of its forests within just 30 years!

indri
Indri indri

babirusa
Babyrousa babyrussa

Pigs in peril!

Within the next few years, the babirusa of the swamp forests of the Sulawesi Archipelago in Indonesia may disappear from the face of Earth forever. When disturbed, the female members of this odd species of wild pig disappear into the dense vegetation of the forest, abandoning their offspring, which have little chance of surviving on their own. In addition to being hunted for its flesh, the babirusa is threatened by the deforestation and mineral prospecting that are destroying its habitat.

23

Declining amphibians

Amphibians are very attached to the humid environments of our planet, and with good reason: it is on the edges of pools, ponds, lakes and swamps that they lay the eggs which become their offspring! Deforestation and the wholesale filling in of wetlands has destroyed an incalculable number of their habitats. Victims of these profound changes in their environment, amphibian populations are declining rapidly throughout the world.

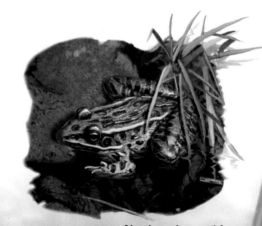

Northern leopard frog
Rana pipiens

Are you curious?

At birth, the tiny panda is very vulnerable. It weighs only 130 grams, or 900 times less than its mother. During the first 4 months of its life, it is carried by its mother, who takes it everywhere she goes. The baby panda is not capable of moving around on its own until about the age of 5 months.

These ones have left us
forever

Scientists estimate that 99% of the species that have ever lived on Earth have succumbed to extinction – a normal part of the evolutionary process. However, in many cases, humans have provoked and accelerated this process. Excessive hunting and fishing, the use of the fur of seals, the big cats and reptiles, the market for ivory and the trade in lucky charms made from the body parts of certain animals have all contributed to the depletion – and in some cases, the outright loss – of certain species of animals.

A lost giant

An ancestor of the modern elephant, the woolly mammoth lived about 10 million years ago on the tundra of the cold regions of Europe, Asia and North America. The victims of a genuine slaughter, these giants, which were over three meters tall, were hunted to excess by prehistoric man, who relished its flesh and used its huge tusks as a building material for their houses.

woolly mammoth
Mammuthus primigenius

dodo
Raphus cucullatus

Dead as a dodo

It took less than 200 years for settlers to wipe out the dodo birds of Mauritius. From the time it was discovered in 1598, this swan-sized bird was hunted not only by humans but also by pigs, dogs and other domestic animals brought to the island. A comical bird that was said to be as dumb as a post, it built its nest right on the ground. Since it was incapable of flying away from its enemies, it's not surprising that it is no longer with us.

The extinction of the great reptiles

Humans are not always responsible for major extinctions. No one is yet certain what caused the disappearance of the dinosaurs. An epidemic? A dramatic change in climate? A volcanic eruption? Today, the most widely accepted explanation is a collision involving a meteorite and the Earth that occurred 65 million years ago. The triceratops, a herbivorous dinosaur whose name means "three-horned face", lived between 65 and 70 million years ago in what is now Canada and the United States. It measured up to 9 meters long and tipped the scales at over 6 tons.

triceratops
Triceratops

great auk
Alca impennis

The last great auk

In 1830, a powerful underwater volcanic eruption swallowed up the small islands on which the great auk, as well as several hundred other birds, once nested. But this natural disaster was not solely responsible for the loss of these large birds. Short-winged and unable to fly, they were slaughtered by the thousands by humans, for their flesh, feathers and fat. The last great auk was killed during an expedition in 1844.

Are you curious?

Several well-preserved mammoths have been found in the frozen ground of Alaska and Siberia. The reddish colour of the fur of these specimens is the result of a chemical reaction involving their hair that occurred after death. Live mammoths actually had black coats.

More clues for
the most curious

ENVIRONMENTS TO SUIT ALL TASTES	
The animals...	**and the difficult conditions they live in**
Petroleum fly larvae (*Psilopa petrolei*)	Oil pools
Brine shrimp (*Artemia salina*)	Salt marshes and salt lakes (the salt content of these environments is twice as high as that of the sea)
Salt creek pupfish (*Cyprinodon salinus*)	Volcanic lake containing no oxygen
Cyclopid copepod (*Thermocyclops schuurmanni*)	
Pupfish (*Cyprinodon macularius*)	Water (49 degrees Celsius)
Mouthbrooder fish (*Tilapia grahami*)	Thermal springs
River trout (*Salmo trutta fario*)	Cold, fast-running water
Black fly larvae (*Simuliidae* family)	
Sea anemone (*Anthozoa* family)	Surf zone
Limpets (*Patella* genus)	
African cave fish (*Caecobarbus geertsi*)	Caves and caverns
Texas blind salamander (*Typhlomolge rathbuni*)	
Golden spider beetle (*Niptus hololeucus*)	Potassium cyanide, cayenne pepper, ammonium chloride
Egyptian nightjar (*Caprimulgus aegyptius*)	Deserts (ground temperatures up to 60 degrees Celsius)
Arctic hare (*Lepus timidus arcticus*)	Polar regions
Emperor penguin (*Aptenodytes forsteri*)	
Ringed seal (*Pusa hispida*)	
Saddleback (*Pagophilus groenlandicus*)	
Jumping spider (*Salticidae* family)	High altitudes (between 6,700 and 7,300 meters)
Luminous shrimp (*Notostomus longirostris*)	Depths of the ocean (deeper than 5,000 meters)

ENDANGERED ANIMALS			
	Animal	**Geographic distribution**	**Natural population**	**Main threats**
Insects	South American longhorn beetle (*Titanus giganteus*)	Brazil	Rare	Destruction of habitat, collectors
	Queen Alexandra's birdwing (*Ornithoptera alexandrae*)	New Guinea	Unknown	Destruction of habitat, collectors
Fish	Common Atlantic sturgeon (*Acipenser sturio*)	Portugal	Unknown	Over-fishing, pollution
	Bluefin tuna (*Thunnus thynnus*)	All oceans	Unknown	Over-fishing, late sexual maturity: 8 years
	Gila trout (*Oncorhynchus gilae*)	United States	Unknown	Pollution
Amphibians and reptiles	Golden toad (*Bufo periglenes*)	Costa Rica	May be extinct	Destruction of habitat
	American crocodile (*Crocodylus acutus*)	Florida, Mexico, South America, Central America and the Caribbean	200 to 300	Destruction of habitat, hunting
	Galapagos giant tortoise (*Geochelone elephantopus*)	Galapagos Islands	2,000	Predators, destruction of habitat
Birds	Mauritius kestrel (*Falco punctatus*)	Mauritius	50 (in 1985)	Destruction of habitat, predators, poisoning
	Siberian white crane (*Grus leucogeranus*)	Siberia, China, Japan	1,400 (in 1985)	Predators, trampling by herds of reindeer
	Crested ibis (*Nipponia nippon*)	Siberia, China, Japan	40 (in 1987)	Destruction of habitat, pollution
	Dalmatian pelican (*Pelecanus crispus*)	Europe, Greece, Turkey, Romania, Romania, former Soviet Union	1,300 couples	Destruction of habitat, predators
Mammals	Black-footed ferret (*Mustela nigripes*)	Wyoming	129 (in 1984)	Destruction of habitat, predators, poisoning, diseases
	Mountain gorilla (*Gorilla gorilla berengei*)	Virunga National Park, Rwanda, Zaire, Uganda	Fewer than 400	Destruction of habitat, poaching and diseases
	Arabian oryx (*Oryx leucoryx*)	Arabia	100	Destruction of habitat
	Black rhinoceros (*Dideros bicornis*)	Sub-Saharan Africa	Fewer than 3,700	Destruction of habitat and poaching
	Tiger (*Panthera tigris*)	Eastern Turkey, Eurasia, Korea	6,000 to 8,000	Hunting, destruction of habitat

For further information...

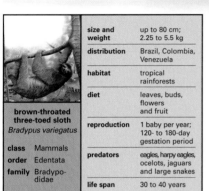

brown-throated three-toed sloth
Bradypus variegatus

size and weight	up to 80 cm; 2.25 to 5.5 kg
distribution	Brazil, Colombia, Venezuela
habitat	tropical rainforests
diet	leaves, buds, flowers and fruit
reproduction	1 baby per year; 120- to 180-day gestation period
predators	eagles, harpy eagles, ocelots, jaguars and large snakes
life span	30 to 40 years

class Mammals
order Edentata
family Bradypodidae

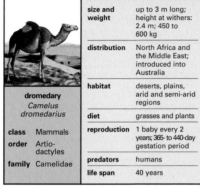

dromedary
Camelus dromedarius

size and weight	up to 3 m long; height at withers: 2.4 m; 450 to 600 kg
distribution	North Africa and the Middle East; introduced into Australia
habitat	deserts, plains, arid and semi-arid regions
diet	grasses and plants
reproduction	1 baby every 2 years; 365- to 440-day gestation period
predators	humans
life span	40 years

class Mammals
order Artiodactyles
family Camelidae

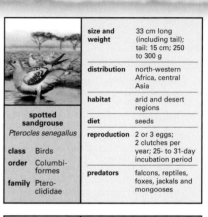

spotted sandgrouse
Pterocles senegallus

size and weight	33 cm long (including tail); tail: 15 cm; 250 to 300 g
distribution	north-western Africa, central Asia
habitat	arid and desert regions
diet	seeds
reproduction	2 or 3 eggs; 2 clutches per year; 25- to 31-day incubation period
predators	falcons, reptiles, foxes, jackals and mongooses

class Birds
order Columbiformes
family Pteroclididae

arctic fox
Alopex lagopus

size and weight	50 to 70 cm; tail: 28 to 40 cm; 3.5 to 8 kg
distribution	northern North America, Europe and Asia
habitat	tundra, arctic regions
diet	voles, lemmings, abandoned carcasses, eggs and small fruit
reproduction	4 to 11 offspring; 49- to 57-day gestation period

class Mammals
order Carnivores
family Canidae

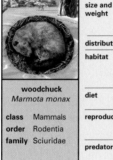

woodchuck
Marmota monax

size and weight	46 to 66 cm; tail: 11 to 16 cm; an average of 2.85 kg
distribution	North America
habitat	fields, hilly areas, edges of wooded areas, sparse forests
diet	plants, insects, young birds
reproduction	1 to 8 offspring; 32-day gestation period
predators	wolves, foxes, buzzards, coyotes, bobcats, humans

class Mammals
order Rodentia
family Sciuridae

viperfish
Chauliodus sloani

size	10 to 30 cm long
distribution	Atlantic, Pacific and Indian Oceans and the Mediterranean Sea
habitat	deep water, depths between 450 and 1,000 m, sometimes up to 2,750 m
diet	leaves, buds, flowers and fruit
reproduction	crustaceans and fish

class Fish
order Stomiiformes
family Chauliodontidae

dipper
Cinclus cinclus

size and weight	17 to 18 cm; 55 to 75 g
distribution	north-western Africa, Europe, central Asia and Anatolia
habitat	swift-running streams and torrents
diet	mollusks, crustaceans, insects, newts and salamanders
reproduction	4 to 6 eggs; 18-day incubation period
predators	weasels, jays, rats and cats

class Birds
order Passeriformes
family Cinclidae

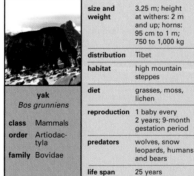

yak
Bos grunniens

size and weight	3.25 m; height at withers: 2 m and up; horns: 95 cm to 1 m; 750 to 1,000 kg
distribution	Tibet
habitat	high mountain steppes
diet	grasses, moss, lichen
reproduction	1 baby every 2 years; 9-month gestation period
predators	wolves, snow leopards, humans and bears
life span	25 years

class Mammals
order Artiodactyla
family Bovidae

blind cave tetra
Astyanax fasciatus mexicanus

size	80 mm
distribution	New Mexico, Texas and Mexico
habitat	underground rivers
diet	invertebrates, fish and aquatic plants

class Fish
order Cypriniformes
family Characidae

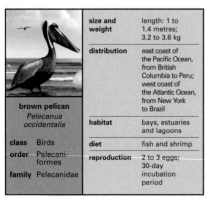

brown pelican
Pelecanus occidentalis

size and weight	length: 1 to 1.4 metres; 3.2 to 3.6 kg
distribution	east coast of the Pacific Ocean, from British Columbia to Peru; west coast of the Atlantic Ocean, from New York to Brazil
habitat	bays, estuaries and lagoons
diet	fish and shrimp
reproduction	2 or 3 eggs; 30-day incubation period

class Birds
order Pelecaniformes
family Pelecanidae

giant panda
Ailuropoda melanoleuca

size and weight	1.2 to 1.6 m long
distribution	China
habitat	mountains on which bamboo grows
diet	bamboo
reproduction	1 baby; 97- to 163-day gestation period
life span	at least 15 years

class Mammals
order Carnivora
family Procyonidae

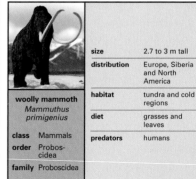

woolly mammoth
Mammuthus primigenius

size	2.7 to 3 m tall
distribution	Europe, Siberia and North America
habitat	tundra and cold regions
diet	grasses and leaves
predators	humans

class Mammals
order Proboscidea
family Proboscidea

Glossary

Abyss

Very deep ocean chasm.

Ambient temperature

Temperature of the immediate surroundings.

Anguilliform

Having a very elongated, eel-like body.

Antarctica

Vast geographical area around the South Pole.

Bed

Natural bottom of a body of water, over which water usually flows.

Blizzard

In northern regions, a strong winter wind accompanied by heavy snow.

Calcareous

Containing calcium carbonate.

Commodity

Something of value, such as food.

Complement

Complete amount, such as the total number of individuals in a group.

Curved

Rounded, shaped like a curve.

Decade

Period of 10 years.

Deforestation

Excessive tree clearing that destroys a forest.

Dehydration

State of a body that has dried out and lost much of the water it contained.

Den

Cavity that serves as a refuge or shelter for a wild animal.

Desert soil

Type of soil that develops in arid climates.

Filling in

Action of adding earth or other material to fill a hole or extend a surface.

Frostbite

Destruction of tissues by freezing, mainly in the nose, fingers and toes.

Gestation

Period during which a female human or animal carries her offspring before birth.

Gill

Organ found on the side of the head of an animal such as a fish that allows it to breathe.

Herbicide

Substance used to control weeds.

Hibernation

State of the body of animals that "sleep" all winter, involving a decline in body temperature and a slowing of metabolic functions.

Hostile

Rendering life very difficult, even seemingly impossible.

Ice floe

In polar regions, huge mass of floating ice.

Inhospitable

Unfriendly, unfavorable to life.

Irreversible

Not able to be reversed or returned to a former state, unidirectional only.

Mineral prospecting

Thorough exploration of an area conducted to locate mineral deposits.

Nosedive

Flying maneuver during which a bird drops headfirst then suddenly uprights itself.

Oasis

Refuge or place of rest, and, in the desert, a place where vegetation can grow due to the presence of water.

Parsimonious

Very cautious when using something so as to save as much as possible.

Passerine

Bird belonging to the Passeriformes order, which includes the sparrow and the chaffinch.

Pesticide

Chemical product used to kill a parasite of any kind that attacks crops.

Quench

Drink to satisfy a thirst.

Residue

What remains or is left over after most of a substance is consumed.

Sheath

Elongated protective covering, like that of a sword.

Stormy

Subject to frequent storms.

Trade

Commerce, or the buying and selling of goods and all related activities.

Translucent

Allowing light to pass through but not transparent enough to allow objects to be seen clearly.

Tundra

Cold region where the vegetation is limited to moss, lichen and a few other plants.

Vent

Vertical channel or conduit that allows substances to rise up and emerge from the surface of the Earth.

Water

Provide with drinking water.

Index

The terms in **bold characters** refer to an illustration; those in *italics* indicate a keyword.

So Many Ways to Live in Difficult Conditions was created and produced by **QA International**, a division of Les Éditions Québec Amérique inc, 329, rue de la Commune Ouest, 3ᵉ étage, Montréal (Québec) H2Y 2E1 Canada **T** 514.499.3000 **F** 514.499.3010
©1999 Éditions Québec Amérique inc.

ISBN 2-89037-978-7

Printed and bound in Canada

10 9 8 7 6 5 4 3 2 1   99